DISCUSSION PAPER 56

PEACE AND SECURITY COOPERATION IN CENTRAL AFRICA

Developments, Challenges and Prospects

ANGELA MEYER

NORDISKA AFRIKAINSTITUTET, UPPSALA 2011

Indexing terms:
Regional organizations
Economic organizations
Regional cooperation
Regional integration
Peacekeeping
Institution building
Regional security
Central Africa

Language checking: Peter Colenbrander
ISSN 1104-8417
ISBN 978-91-7106-693-0
© The author and Nordiska Afrikainstitutet 2011
Production: Byrå4
Print on demand, Lightning Source UK Ltd.

Contents

Glossary

ACBF	African Capacity Building Fund
AEC	African Economic Community
AEF	Federation of French Equatorial Africa/ Afrique équatoriale française
APRD	Popular Army for the Restoration of the Republic and Democracy/ Armée populaire pour la restauration de la République et la démocratie
ASF	African Standby Force
AU	African Union
AU-PSC	African Union Peace and Security Council
BDEAC	Central African States Development Bank/ Banque de développement des Etats de l'Afrique centrale
BEAC	Bank of Central African States/ Banque des Etats de l'Afrique centrale
CAR	Central African Republic
CEMAC	Economic and Monetary Community of Central Africa/ Communauté économique et monétaire de l'Afrique centrale
CEN-SAD	Community of Sahel-Saharan States
CDS	Commission for Defence and Security
CEPGL	Economic Community of the Great Lakes Countries
CEWS	Continental Early Warning System
COMESA	Common Market for Eastern and Southern Africa
COPAX	Council for Peace and Security in Central Africa/ Conseil de paix et de sécurité en Afrique centrale
CSO	Civil Society Organisation
DDR	Disarmament, Demobilisation and Reintegration
DRC	Democratic Republic of Congo
EAC	East African Community
EASBRICOM	East Africa Standby Brigade Coordination Mechanism
EC	European Commission
ECCAS	Economic Community of Central African States/ Communauté économique des Etats de l'Afrique centrale (CEEAC)
ECOWAS	Economic Community of Western African States
EPA	Economic Partnership Agreements
FACA	Central African Armed Forces/ Forces armées centrafricaines
FOMAC	Central African Multinational Force/ Force Multinationale de l'Afrique Centrale
FOMUC	Multinational Force in the Central African Republic/ Force Multinationale en Centrafrique

ICG	International Crisis Group
IGAD	Intergovernmental Authority on Development
MARAC	Central African Early-Warning System/ *Mécanisme* d'alerte rapide en Afrique centrale
MICOPAX	Mission for the Consolidation of Peace in the Central African Republic/ Mission de consolidation de la Paix en République centrafricaine
MINURCA	United Nations Mission in the Central African Republic/ Mission des Nations Unies en République centrafricaine
MISAB	Inter-African Mission to Monitor the Implementation of the Bangui *Agreements*/ Mission interafricaine de surveillance des Accords de Bangui
MLC	Movement for the Liberation of Congo/ Mouvement pour la Libération du Congo
NARC	North Africa Regional Capability
OAU	Organisation of African Unity
PAPS- CEEAC	ECCAS Support Programme for Peace and Security/ Programme d'appui en matière de paix et sécurité de la CEEAC
PREGESCO	Capacity building project for civil society organizations in conflict prevention and management in Central Africa/ Projet de renforcement des capacités des organisations de la société civile dans la prévention et la gestion des conflits en Afrique Centrale
PSO	Peace Support Operation
RECAMP	Reinforcement Of African *Peace*-Keeping Capacities/ Renforcement des Capacités Africaines de maintien de la paix
REPAC	Central African Network of Parliamentarians/ Réseau des Parlementaires de l'Afrique centrale
SADC	Southern African Development Community
SADC-CNGO	Southern African Development Community Council of Non Governmental Organizations
SERACOB	Service for the Reinforcement of Assistance to Grassroots Communities in Central Africa/ Service de renforcement des appuis aux communautés de base en Afrique centrale
SSR	Security Sector Reform
TCI	Community Integration Tax/ Taxe communautaire d'intégration
UDEAC	Central African Customs Union/ Union douanière des Etats de l'Afrique centrale

UEAC	Central African Economic Union/ Union économique de l'Afrique centrale
UFDR	Union of the Democratic Forces for Unity/ Union des forces démocratiques pour le rassemblement
UMA	Arab Maghreb Union/ Union du Maghreb Arabe
UMAC	Central African Monetary Union/ Union monétaire de l'Afrique centrale
UN	United Nations
WACSOF	West African Civil Society Forum

Foreword

This Discussion Paper explores regional peace and security cooperation in Central Africa. It focuses on the expansion of the agenda of regional economic communities in Central Africa to include peace and security issues. Of note is the analysis of the evolution of the Economic Community of Central African States (ECCAS) and the Economic and Monetary Community of Central Africa (CEMAC) and the formation two regional peace missions, FOMUC and MICOPAX. The paper is framed by the formation of Central Africa's regional response to the changing global context of international peacekeeping and the emergence of "African solutions to African conflicts" as part of the new AU peace and security architecture, as well as by the threats posed by violent conflicts in the Central African Republic. Other factors include the need to address the spill-over effects of intra-state conflicts in the region, and the role of the international community, particularly France. The emergence of FOMUC and MICOPAX in the context of Central Africa's peace and security architecture receives critical and detailed attention, providing an analysis of the role of various actors, and the new trend in regional cooperation in Africa, where regional economic communities have increasingly taken on security roles. In this regard, the discussion of FOCUC and MICOPAX is linked to the challenges confronting peace and security in Central Africa. Issues discussed include the crisis of governance leading to political instability, paradoxical poverty within resource-rich member states, low levels of intra-regional economic growth and trade, poor funding for and weak capacity of regional institutions and peace operations. Others include overlapping memberships in different regional economic communities by states in the region, the lack of commitment by leaders of member states to a constructive vision of regional cooperation, the pursuit of competing national and selfish political interests at the regional level by such leaders, problems related to the absence of a clear regional leadership, the marginal role of civil society in regional peace and security institutions, and interference by foreign powers, particularly France. The author demonstrates how and to what degree CEMAC and ECCAS have addressed these challenges, and identifies and evaluates the supporting role of the international community. The paper is, however, clear in concluding that international partners should support only more democratic and effective forms of integration that give primacy to development and human security for the people of the region. This Discussion Paper is an important resource for those scholars, policy-makers, journalists and activists interested in gaining first-hand knowledge of the peace and security challenges of Central Africa.

Cyril Obi
Senior Researcher
The Nordic Africa Institute

Abstract

This paper provides a critical appraisal of regional peace and security cooperation in Central Africa. Since gaining their independence in the 1960s, Central African states have agreed to strengthen their cooperation at the regional level. Although the initial focus was on regional economic cooperation and trade, growing crises and conflicts in the region led to security issues becoming an important element in regional agreements and activities. The paper analyses the progressive transformation of the agendas of two Central African economic communities, the Economic and Monetary Community of Central Africa and the Economic Community of Central African States, from purely economic matters to the inclusion of security cooperation. Particular attention is given to the crises in the Central African Republic, a major context for two regional peace missions, *Force Multinationale en Centrafrique* and *Mission de consolidation de la Paix en République centrafricaine*. It also examines Central African peace and security architecture and outlines major peace and security challenges confronting the sub-region.

Introduction

Since the late 1990s and early 2000s, two regional economic communities, the Economic and Monetary Community of Central Africa (CEMAC) and the Economic Community of Central African States (ECCAS), have increasingly addressed peace and security issues by responding to conflicts in the region. This development can be gleaned from the formation of the *Force Multinationale en Centrafrique* (FOMUC), a peacekeeping mission deployed by CEMAC members in the Central African Republic (CAR) from 2002 to 2008. At the same time, ECCAS was busy establishing the Central African peace and security architecture by forming several instruments and mechanisms for conflict prevention. Since July 2008, ECCAS has taken over command of FOMUC and transformed it into the *Mission de consolidation de la Paix en République centrafricaine* (MICOPAX).

This paper critically appraises regional peace and security cooperation in Central Africa, particularly the regional peacekeeping missions consecutively deployed by CEMAC and ECCAS in the CAR. It posits that without moving beyond the current form and level of intergovernmental cooperation, attaining the goal of sustainable regional security will continue to be a potent challenge for the region. Solutions discussed in this context include greater commitment by member states, empowerment of supranational institutions and involvement of non-state actors in regional peace and security processes.

The paper is structured in seven sections. The introduction is followed by overview of the historical background to regional economic, and security cooperation by the two Central African communities, ECCAS and CEMAC. The third section sheds light on Central Africa's emerging peace and security architecture, while the fourth addresses the activities of FOMUC and MICOPAX, Central Africa's first regional peace operations and response to growing insecurity in the CAR. The section that follows examines the major peace and security challenges facing the region, while the sixth address the pros and cons of regional peacekeeping in Central Africa. In the final section, the prospects for improving Central African regional peace and security efforts are critically explored.

ECCAS and CEMAC: The New Trend Towards Regional Security Cooperation

There are three regional communities in Central Africa, each pursuing rather similar goals: strengthening economic cooperation between their member states and promoting economic development in the region. CEMAC has the longest history, being an offshoot of the Central African Customs Union UDEAC, which was established in 1966. On the other hand, ECCAS is the largest in terms of number of member states (10) and geographical coverage (6, 640, 600 square kilometres). The third, and smallest, regional community is the Economic Community of the Great Lakes Countries (CEPGL). CEPGL has been constrained by the conflicts that have adversely affected relations between its three member states, Democratic Republic of Congo (DRC), Rwanda and Burundi. As a consequence, its activities have been rather limited.

Although all three communities initially had purely economic objectives, the scope of Central African regional cooperation has progressively widened to include peace and security issues. Whereas the CEPGL is still struggling with post-conflict reconstruction challenges, the members of CEMAC and ECCAS have since the late 1990s, and to a greater or lesser degree, undertaken joint initiatives for the settlement and prevention of conflicts.[1]

ECCAS: Setting new priorities for regional cooperation

ECCAS was created in 1983. Its 10 member states are Cameroon, Gabon, CAR, Chad, Republic of the Congo, Equatorial Guinea, Burundi, DRC, Angola and São Tomé and Principe. ECCAS has overlapping memberships with a number of other African regional communities. For instance, Cameroon, Gabon, CAR, Chad, Republic of the Congo and Equatorial Guinea also belong to CEMAC. Burundi and DRC are also members of CEPGL and of the Common Market for Eastern and Southern Africa (COMESA). In addition, Burundi has joined the East African Community (EAC), while Angola and DRC are also part of the Southern African Development Community (SADC). Difficulties in managing multiple memberships in four regional communities – COMESA, EAC, CEPGL and ECCAS – were among the main reasons Rwanda, one of ECCAS's founding members, quit the community in 2007.

ECCAS was founded as one of the pillars of the African Economic Commu-

---

1. The paper concentrates on CEMAC and ECCAS and does not include an analysis of CE-PGL. This is partly due to the weak performance of the latter, still in reconstruction. The paper pays particular attention to recent regional peacekeeping initiatives in the CAR involving CEMAC and ECCAS.

nity (AEC), in the context of the 1980 Lagos Plan of Action.[2] Its original target was to prepare at the regional level for the continental economic integration of Africa and the establishment of an African Common Market by 2000. Consequently, it was directed at facilitating self-sustaining development in Central Africa "in order to achieve collective self-reliance, raise the standard of living of its peoples, increase and maintain economic stability, foster close and peaceful relations between Member States and contribute to the progress and development of the African continent."[3] Its founding treaty of 1983 foresees the establishment of a single regional market, including the abolition of tariff and non-tariff barriers; establishing a common external customs tariff and common trade policy towards third countries; progressive achievement of the free movement of persons, goods, services and capital; as well as harmonisation of national policies in a number of fields, such as industry, transport, energy and agriculture.

Initially, ECCAS performed very poorly. The community's progress was largely impeded by financial and technical bottlenecks resulting from the failure of member states to pay their fees regularly and to provide sufficient resources and capacities. As a result, contacts with AEC remained undeveloped. In addition, the conflicts that affected most member states during the 1990s paralysed economic cooperation and exchange within the community. Between 1992 and 1998, the community's activities were disrupted and the headquarters in Libreville, the Gabonese capital, remained non-operational.

At the extraordinary summit in February 1998 in Libreville, Central African heads of state announced their decision to revive ECCAS and give new impetus to their cooperation. Consequently, the community embarked on wide-ranging institutional reform and revision of its agenda. Formal contacts with AEC were re-established and the importance of ECCAS as a major economic community in Central Africa was confirmed on the continental level. The promotion of economic cooperation and development through the progressive creation of a single Central African market was retained as the central aim.

The lessons from of years of conflict and crises made it clear that regional economic cooperation could not succeed without regional peace and security. As a result, ECCAS's mandate was broadened to include the joint promotion of

---

2. The Lagos Plan of Action for the Economic Development of Africa, 1980-2000, backed by the OAU, was endorsed in April 1980 by several African political leaders. It aims to increase Africa's development and self-sufficiency by promoting economic development at the regional level. The plan was built on several regional pillars. This task was given to the Economic Community of West African States (ECOWAS), in Eastern and Southern Africa to the Preferential Trade Area (PTA) (later COMESA) and the Southern African Development Coordination Conference (SADCC) (later SADC), and in Northern Africa to the Maghreb Arab Union (UMA). ECCAS was created as the Central African pillar.
3. *Treaty establishing the Economic Community of Central African States* (Libreville, 1983): Article 4.

peace, security and stability in the sub-region. At the 10th heads of state summit in Malabo, Equatorial Guinea's capital, in June 2002, the development of capacities to maintain peace, security and stability as essential prerequisites for economic and social development were listed among ECCAS's new priorities.[4]

The revival of ECCAS led to the reconstruction of its institutional architecture. The conference of heads of state remains the community's main decision-making body. It defines the policy direction of the organisation, and is assisted by the council of ministers. This council meets twice a year and makes recommendations and gives advice on the achievement of the community's goals and objectives. The central administrative organ is the secretariat in Libreville, headed by a secretary-general, who is in charge of implementing the decisions of the conference of heads of state and the council of ministers. Although the 1983 treaty foresaw the creation of an ECCAS regional court of justice, this has not yet happened. In addition, the community's Network of Parliamentarians (REPAC) is currently in the process of being established.

As a result of the new focus on security, several additional organs and mechanisms have been created. These include the Council for Peace and Security in Central Africa (COPAX), created in February 1999 to promote, maintain and consolidate peace and security in the area covered by ECCAS. The COPAX protocol was adopted in 2000 and its standing orders in June 2002. Article 4 of its protocol mainly defines COPAX's objectives in the field of preventing, managing and settling conflicts; reducing tensions and preventing armed conflicts; developing confidence-building measures between member states; promoting peaceful dispute-resolution measures; and facilitating mediation efforts in crises and conflicts between member states and with third parties (ECCAS 2010).

COPAX has three key technical organs. The Commission for Defence and Security (CDS) brings together member states' chiefs of staff and commanders-in-chief of police and gendarmerie forces. It advises the conference of heads of state on security and defence issues as well as on the organisation of any joint military operations. The Central African Early Warning System (MARAC) collects and analyses data for the early detection and prevention of conflicts and crises. The Central African Multinational Force (FOMAC) is a non-permanent peace-support operation comprising contingents from member states for regional peacekeeping and peace-support. The protocol establishing COPAX was officially ratified in January 2004 and the new organs and mechanisms have been progressively put in place. This broadening of ECCAS's institutional structure to include defence and security institutions and mechanisms was undertaken in coordination with the African Union's (AU) efforts to define a common peace

---

4. The other three priorities being developing physical, economic and monetary integration; developing a culture of human integration; and establishing an autonomous financing mechanism for ECCAS.

and security policy and set up an African peace and security architecture built on regional pillars.

CEMAC: Regional Response to security challenges

CEMAC is a relatively young organisation, but with old roots. It is the successor to the Central African customs union, *Union Douanière des Etats de l'Afrique Centrale* (UDEAC), created in 1966 by five member states to maintain the colonial-era economic ties among them. UDEAC's initial members were Cameroon, Gabon, Chad, Republic of Congo and CAR. To achieve its objectives, UDEAC foresaw progressive harmonisation of taxes and duties and establishment of a common external tariff. It was joined in 1984 by Equatorial Guinea.

Despite early achievements and the existence of a common monetary unit, the CFA franc, UDEAC's operational capabilities were very poor. A growing lack of commitment by member states, irregular payment of contributions and the economic crises of the 1980s led to financial shortages and hindered the proper functioning of the community and achievement of targets and objectives. Over the years, members' interest in regional policies and activities diminished progressively and intraregional trade remained low. By the late 1980s, the regionalisation process was more or less stagnant.

The decision to reactivate regional cooperation by creating a new community on the foundations of UDEAC is in line with the "second wave of regionalisation" that swept the African continent during the 1990s. During this period, several regionalisation initiatives were revived and new ones launched. In Central Africa, the six UDEAC partners agreed in 1994 to undertake a comprehensive reform process and in 1999 CEMAC was formally established as UDEAC's successor by the N'Djaména Treaty. The main objective of CEMAC is to monitor and promote convergence in national economic policies, coordinate sectoral policies and progressively create a single market.

The community is based on four main institutions. The monetary union, UMAC, is built on the common CFA franc, introduced into French-speaking Central African colonies in 1945 by France. UMAC defines and monitors members' monetary policies. The economic union, UEAC, is still developing the process that is expected to lead to the eventual free movement of goods, services, capital and persons. Till now, despite a comprehensive body of legislation, the implementation of different steps towards a Central African economic union has been slower than planned. The two other main CEMAC institutions are the court of justice in N'Djaména and the parliament, which was established in Malabo in August 2010.

As with ECCAS, the main decision-making powers lie with members' political leaders, who meet once a year in a conference of heads of state. The main function of this conference is to determine the major orientations of the community and its institutions. It also decides upon the heads of most community institutions. Member states' ministers of financial and economic issues meet regularly in two ministerial councils to guide and monitor the advancement of UEAC and UMAC. All institutions are assisted by a community secretariat, based in Bangui, CAR's capital. In 2007, the secretariat underwent comprehensive reform and was transformed into a commission, based on the example of the European Union (EU). The commission is led by a president and currently comprises four commissioners dealing with different policy fields: the common market; infrastructure and sustainable development; human rights and good governance; and economic and monetary policies. Commissioners are appointed by the conference of heads of state for four years, renewable for a second term.

Like ECCAS, CEMAC seeks to promote economic cooperation and development among its member states. In response to the growing insecurity and instability in the CAR, the community in 2002 decided to intervene and set up a regional peace force, FOMUC. Since ECCAS's reform process had not been completed by the end of 2002, it decided to join the FOMUC mission as part of CEMAC, pending the full operationalisation of its own newly created security mechanisms. FOMUC was deployed to Bangui in December 2002 and remained in the CAR for almost six years. It was replaced in July 2008 by MICOPAX, when CEMAC transferred authority for the regional peace operation to ECCAS. Since July 2008, CEMAC has again concentrated on trade and economic cooperation. It appears that its resort to peace and security activities was more on an ad hoc than a sustained basis.

Central African Peace and Security Architecture

The establishment of joint regional security institutions, mechanisms and operations and the conduct of peace and security activities in Central Africa reflect a general trend in the approach to security on the African continent. This trend was mainly prompted by the growing unwillingness of the international community during the 1990s to intervene actively in international conflicts (Kurth 2005). The major reasons for this reluctance can be found in changing global interests and a new focus by the international community on developments in Asia and Eastern Europe. Moreover, in the case of Africa, the inauspicious US intervention in Somalia heightened the reluctance of Western governments to send their own ground troops to the continent for peacekeeping. An additional explanation in the case of France was the significant change in political personnel that induced comprehensive reform of France's Africa policy (Gounin 2009).

As a consequence of this "intervention fatigue" the international community, and first and foremost the United Nations, emphasised the important role and responsibility of regional organisations in conflict management and promoted increased burden-sharing.[5] In this changing context, African states were urged to strengthen their conflict-resolving capacities. The new emphasis on "Africanisation" and "African ownership" initiated a so-called "African Renaissance". The concept of "African solutions to African problems", coined in 1998 by Thabo Mbeki, found expression in the progressive strengthening of the security role of hitherto exclusively economic communities.[6] This development was moreover strengthened by a certain willingness of the international community to support regional security initiatives and operations financially and/or logistically, as long as they were carried out by African regional organisations.

Several African regional communities, such as the Economic Community of Western African States (ECOWAS) and SADC,[7] had set up regional security mechanisms and launched joint operations as early as the 1990s (Obi 2010, Schleicher 2004, Schoeman and Muller 2010). Following the transformation of the Organisation of African Unity (OAU) into the AU in 2002, the AU Peace and Security Council (AU-PSC) was officially created in May 2004. The PSC is the central organ in the AU's peace and security architecture. In the declaration of the AU summit of African heads of state, "the establishment of the [PSC] marks an historic watershed in Africa's progress towards resolving its conflicts and the building of a durable peace and security order."[8] The PSC is the standing decision-making organ for the prevention, management and resolution of conflicts. Its main aim is facilitating timely and efficient responses to conflicts and crises in Africa. Besides the PSC, the other pillars of the AU's peace and security architecture are the Panel of the Wise, the Continental Early Warning System (CEWS) and a peace fund. The PSC is regionally embedded, with

---

5. In 1995, UN Secretary-General Boutros Ghali, remarked: "The founders of the United Nations, in Chapter VIII of the Charter of the United Nations, envisaged an important role for regional organizations in the maintenance of international peace and security. It is increasingly apparent that the United Nations cannot address every potential and actual conflict troubling the world. Regional or subregional organizations sometimes have a comparative advantage in taking the lead role in the prevention and settlement of conflicts and to assist the United Nations in containing them." In: United Nations, *Improving Preparedness for Conflict Prevention and Peace-keeping in Africa: Report of the Secretary General*, UN Doc. A/50/711-S/1995/911, 01.11.1995 http://www.un.org/documents/ga/docs/50/plenary/a50-711.htm (accessed April 25, 2009).

6. Thabo Mbeki, *The African Renaissance*, Statement of Deputy President Thabo Mbeki, SABC, Gallagher Estate, August 13, 1998.

7. In 1996, SADC set up the Organ on Politics, Defence and Security Cooperation (OPDS). Mainly due to disagreement among member states on its status and authority within the SADC, OPDS became operational only in 2001, with the ratification of the Protocol on Politics, Defence and Security Cooperation. In 1998, some SADC's member states carried out joint military interventions in Lesotho and the DRC, but the status of these operations as SADC missions is much debated, as they were not supported by all SADC members.

8. African Union, *Statement of Commitment to Peace And Security in Africa, issued by the Heads of State and Government of the Member States of the Peace and Security Council of the African Union*, Addis Ababa, May 25, 2004. Article 1.

its components supported by bodies and mechanisms in several regional communities. The Panel of the Wise, which advises the PSC and plays a conflict-prevention and peacemaking role, is composed of five persons representing the African regions. CEWS and its observation and monitoring centre (Situation Room) work in close cooperation with regional monitoring centres that collect and provide data for analysis and evaluation (Fanta 2009).

As the central peacekeeping instrument, an African Standby Force (ASF) is to conduct African peace operations on the continent. ASF will rely on five standby brigades of 3,000 to 5,000 troops each, to be set up on the regional level in Northern, Eastern, Western, Central and Southern Africa. Headquarters, planning elements and logistics are to be based in the regions.[9]

Regional organisations contributing to the African peace architecture are the Arab Maghreb Union (UMA), the Community of Sahel-Saharan States (CEN-SAD), COMESA, EAC, ECOWAS, the Inter-governmental Authority on Development (IGAD), SADC, and, for Central Africa ECCAS. Parts of ASF are also to be formed by the East Africa Standby Brigade Coordination Mechanism (EASBRICOM) and the North Africa Regional Capability (NARC), which are managed by regional economic communities.

In Central Africa, ECCAS's efforts to set up a regional peace and security architecture largely respond to developments on the continental level. Whereas the early warning system of MARAC is one of the pillars of CEWS, FOMAC is intended to contribute to the ASF. A memorandum of understanding has been adopted between representatives of the AU and ECCAS, as well as of the other regional communities and organs contributing to the African peace and security architecture.[10] Progress with these regional contributions to African peace and security architecture differs greatly across the continent.

In Central Africa, MARAC has been progressively put in place in recent years. Especially since 2007, major capacity-building efforts have been made, notably with the support of the EU. The EU-ECCAS Support Programme for Peace and Security in Central Africa (PAPS) has been assisting the community to fully develop its capacity to provide regional peace and security. To facilitate MARAC's operations and implementation of operational guidelines elaborated by the ECCAS secretariat, regular workshops have been organised in the ECCAS member states. Examples include those held in September 2007 in Libre-

---

9. See: African Union, *Protocol framework for the Establishment of the African Standby Force and the Military Staff Committee, Document adopted by the Third Meeting of African Chiefs of Defence Staff*, Addis Ababa, May 15-16, 2003.

10. African Union, *Memorandum of Understanding on Cooperation in the area of Peace and Security between the African Union, the Regional Economic Communities and the Coordinating Mechanisms of the Regional Standby Brigades of Eastern Africa and Northern Africa*. Online available: http://www.africa-union.org/root/AU/AUC/Departments/PSC/ps/PSC%20Publications/MOU_AU_RECs_E.pdf (accessed November 1, 2010).

ville (Gabon) and in December 2007 in Kinshasa (DRC). Since May 2008, MARAC has carried out regular early warning and conflict analyses. Data collection is organised by an observation centre in Libreville and decentralised bureaux in member states, of which five have already been created (ECCAS 2010).

A persistent problem is the mechanism's weak analytical capacities. This needs to be addressed to ensure that member states can effectively contribute to monitoring the crises, conflicts and conflict risks within the region. The challenges to the efficiency of the mechanism include the joint elaboration of the indicators to enable early detection of potential threats, as well as the need to find a common language and understanding and to determine observation priorities to guide monitoring activities. Also crucial is the need to guarantee the smooth transfer of data and efficient cooperation between the different elements and levels of MARAC. In other words, the efficiency and speed of the processes to detect risks and respond to threats need to be ensured. Thus, the distribution of responsibilities among actors and centres on the local, national, regional and continental levels must be strengthened. As the function of MARAC is limited to detecting threats and issuing warnings, much apparently depends on the willingness of the states to heed these alerts and react appropriately.

The establishment of the Central African brigade as part of the ASF is under way. According to the standing order of 2002, FOMAC is a "force composed of national inter-service, police and gendarmerie contingents and of civil modules from Member States of the ECCAS, with a view to carrying our peace, security and humanitarian assistance missions."[11] Over the years, several multinational military exercises have been carried out with a view to building and institutionalising the Central African force. In June 2010, a major exercise, "Kwanza 2010", took place in Angola. Involving 3,700 troops from Central African national armies, police and gendarmerie, civilian components and Non-Governmental Organisations (NGOs), it included air, sea and ground operations (ECCAS 2010). According to ECCAS Secretary-General Louis Sylvain-Goma, while the exercise showed that 75 per cent of objectives had been achieved,[12] the constitution of the force depends above all on the political will and commitment of members states. The establishment of FOMAC and the regional brigade has been seriously affected by financial and logistical difficulties and lack of capacities. An additional problem is the still underdeveloped civil component of the force. Although FOMAC's standing orders include a "civilian module" alongside the military and police component, the involvement of or cooperation with civilians

11. ECCAS, *Standing Orders of the Central African Multinational Force*, 2002.
12. Jean-Marie Nkambua, "Maintien de la Paix: La CEEAC se dote d'une force multinationale d'Afrique centrale (FOMAC)", *L'avenir Quotidien*, June 7, 2010.

remain weak. The primary role of the civil element in a mission is to carry out all administrative tasks and to prepare for monitoring elections.

Article 3 of the mission's mandate also includes activities in the political, judicial and penal fields as well as for the protection of human rights and issues related to children, gender and the fight against HIV/AIDS.[13] Strengthening FOMAC's civilian module and including civil actors in MICOPAX requires the selection of appropriate personnel and their training. Here, developments have been rather slow. However, progress has so far been made in creating the post of special representative who, in terms of article 5 of MICOPAX's mandate, acts as a link between the mission and local reality, and ensures the relationship between troops and the population.

FOMUC and MICOPAX: Central Africa's first regional peace missions

FOMUC was the first initiative by Central African states to carry out a joint peace mission in a member state. The major reason for the CEMAC states' decision of October 2002 to carry out such a mission was the ever worsening security situation in the CAR.

Slightly larger than France, but with a population of just 4.5 million and located right in the centre of the African continent, CAR is one of the poorest countries in the world. A former French colony, its postcolonial history has often been described as turbulent, or even ludicrous ("*ubuesque*") and "chaotic" (Balencie and de la Grange 2001). Harelimana even considers the country's fragility, particularly critical for state institutions and the political process, as one of its main characteristics (Harelimana 2008). Indeed, the first three decades after independence in 1960 saw a succession of relatively long-lived regimes, including an empire, all of which were violently overthrown.[14] Since the 1990s, the political situation has remained particularly precarious, with a series of attempted and successful coups d'état. France continued to have considerable influence on CAR's politics as well as on the security situation and stability. For Paris, CAR occupied a geostrategic position in Africa even after 1960: with the retention of the two permanent military bases of Bouar and Camp Béal, it remained the "hub" of France's military presence on the continent (Faes and Smith 2000).

---

13. CEEAC, *13ème Session Ordinaire de la Conférence des Chefs d'Etats et de Gouvernement ; Décision /CEEAC/CCEG /XIII/08, Portant Mandat de la Mission de Paix du 12 juillet au 31 décembre2008 et Mission de Consolidation de la Paix du 1er janvier 2009 aux environs de l'année 2013 du Conseil de Paix et de Sécurité de l'Afrique Centrale en République Centrafricaine*, June 12, 2008 (Article 3).

14. Regimes in the CAR from 1960 until 1993: David Dacko (1960-66, removed by coup d'état); Jean-Bédel Bokassa (1966–76, transformed into an empire in 1976), Bokassa I (1976–79, removed in 1979 by French-led military intervention "Opération Barracuda'); David Dacko (1979–81, removed by coup d'état), André Kolingba (1986–93).

French influence was, moreover, apparent in its involvement in the CAR's domestic politics and in the country's political and regime changes. Without doubt, the most striking example of intervention was "Operation Barracuda," in 1979, described by French diplomat Jacques Foccart as "France's last colonial expedition" (Glaser and Smith 2006). Organised by the French secret service and conducted by Special Forces, the operation aimed to topple Emperor Bokassa and bring David Dacko to power as his successor. Even when France's role in the putsch became public, the violation of the CAR's sovereignty rights was not discussed (Jean 2008). For the Central African political elites, the continued influence of the former colonial power presented a welcome opportunity to gain access to extraordinary financial and military support and, at the same time, to bolster their weak legitimacy (Binoua 2005). The changes in external support and decrease in French backing revealed both the weakness of the CAR's political system and the fragility and vulnerability of the country's social and political order.

The progressive withdrawal of France and reduction of its activities and military presence in the CAR in the mid-1990s was in line with the general reorientation of France's Africa policy, especially under the government of Lionel Jospin, elected in 1997 (Marchesin 1998, Gounin 2009).[15] The main change was a gradual reduction of French troops and the closing in 1997 of the two military bases in CAR. In 1998, the French government launched the capacity-building programme *Renforcement des Capacités Africaines de Maintien de la Paix* (RE-CAMP), as a middle way between "intervention" and "indifference."[16]

In April, May and November 1996, CAR was shaken by a series of army mutinies, mainly triggered by grievances over non-payment of salary arrears and ethnic favouritism. This situation was further compounded by the activities of several rebel militia groups seeking to topple the government. The crisis could only be settled with external support, with France once again playing a central role. Since 1997, several multinational peace operations have been deployed to the CAR in response to the volatile security situation and the inability of CAR's then-president, Ange-Felix Patassé, to deal with the growing risk of civil war.

The first intervention was the *Mission Inter-Africaine de Surveillance des Accords de Bangui* (MISAB), set up by a mediation committee comprising heads of state from Gabon, Burkina Faso, Mali and Chad. The mission's task was to

---

15. Since the mid-1990s, France has begun to replace its policy of military presence and direct involvement in Africa by a policy of capacity building and training to strengthen African military forces. This decision was based on several factors, including a new global turning towards new and emerging markets, reinforcement of relations between the EU and Africa (partly replacing bilateral cooperation), as well as budgetary factors and new French geopolitical interests. See Gounin 2009.

16. Allusion to the 1997 statement of then-Prime Minister Lionel Jospin "Neither interference nor indifference." ("Ni ingérence ni indifférence").

restore calm after the mutinies, supervise the disarmament of rebels and militias and to monitor the implementation of a peace agreement between the government and rebels. MISAB was composed of a total of 800 troops from Burkina Faso, Chad, Gabon, Mali, Senegal and Togo and under Gabonese command. Financial and logistical support was provided by France under the RECAMP programme. In addition, the mission was backed by resolution 1136 (1997) of the UN Security Council and chapter VII of the UN Charter.

In January 1998, France's decision to cut support to MISAB in line with its efforts to reduce its military presence in the CAR led to calls for a review of the mission. Under pressure from France, the Security Council decided in March 1998 by resolution 1159 (1998) to replace the inter-African mission with a UN operation, the *Mission des Nations Unies en République centrafricaine* (MINUR-CA). The decision was intended to prevent the creation of a vacuum by the withdrawal of international troops in the CAR in advance of parliamentary and presidential elections scheduled for late 1998 and October 1999. MINURCA deployed to Bangui in April 1998 and comprised 1,350 troops. Besides monitoring the elections, MINURCA's mandate was to consolidate security, stability and free movement in and around the capital, control and supervise disarmament and reform and strengthen national police forces. After four extensions of its initial three-month mandate, the operation ended in February 2000.

FOMUC and MICOPAX: Two Central African peace missions

Security and stability remained volatile in the CAR after the withdrawal of the two international operations. Only with the support of external forces did President Patassé avert several attempted coups d'état. In May 2001 and October 2002, Libya sent troops to the CAR under the umbrella of CEN-SAD. During 2002, Patassé received additional support from Congolese rebel leader Jean-Pierre Bemba (Mehler 2001). Bemba's troops, the *Mouvement pour la Libération du Congo* (MLC), however, committed serious human rights violations that increased the insecurity (Mehler 2008).

In October 2002, CEMAC heads of state announced the deployment of a joint peace operation to the CAR. FOMUC was composed of 380 troops, who were initially based in Bangui. During the first four months of its deployment in December 2002, FOMUC was mandated to protect President Patassé's government against further coups and rebellions and secure the capital and its airport. However, its size largely limited the mission's ability to act. When former armed forces Chief of Staff François Bozizé again tried in March 2003 to seize power in Bangui, FOMUC could not prevent the toppling of the president. Bozizé's violent coming to power necessitated complete revision of FOMUC's mandate.

The mission's core responsibility remained restoration and consolidation of peace, security and stability in CAR. In addition, FOMUC was largely involved in monitoring the transition and reconciliation process launched by Bozizé. It also assisted in the preparations for elections in May 2005. The initial focus on the capital was progressively widened. In summer 2006, two units of 80 troops each were dispatched to the cities of Bria in the northeast and Bozoum in the northwest when military activities by armed rebel movements intensified in the surrounding provinces. An additional contingent of 119 Cameroonian soldiers was dispatched in March 2008 to Paoua, close to the border with Cameroon. By the end of the mission in July 2008, the task force's total capacity was 500 troops (African Union 2008). However, between 2002 and 2004, major financial, logistical and technical support was provided by France. Since 2004, with the creation of the African Peace Facility Programme, large parts of FOMUC's budget have been covered by the EU, whereas logistical and military assistance still mainly came from France. In contrast, CEMAC's financial contribution to the operation was marginal.[17]

In October 2007, the Central African heads of state agreed to transfer supervisory authority of their joint peace mission in the CAR from CEMAC to ECCAS. By then, the process of setting up ECCAS's peace and security architecture had progressed. The transfer of authority mirrored the Central African states' commitment to coordinate the responsibilities of the two regional communities CEMAC and ECCAS, and to increasingly focus ECCAS on security issues.

The budget of MICOPAX, which took over from FOMUC in July 2008, is still mainly covered by the European Commission (EC). For 2009, the EC granted funding of € 14.6 million for troop allowances and general maintenance.[18] A further € 9.5 million was provided bilaterally by France in 2009. Of the budget, 20 per cent is supposed to be provided at the community level.

Compared to FOMUC, the new mission has more personnel. In 2010, 527 troops were contributed primarily by Cameroon, Gabon, Chad and the DRC. In contrast to FOMUC, MICOPAX's mandate also foresees inclusion of a police and a civil element. Whereas 146 policemen and 21 military police have already joined the operation, the civil component is still being assembled and has not been fully deployed.[19]

---

17. See also: *"EU relations with the Central African Republic"* published on the Website of the European Commission under:
    http://ec.europa.eu/development/geographical/regionscountries/countries/country_profile.c fm?cid=cf&type=long&lng=en(accessed September 26, 2010).

18. Communiqués de Presse, *Signature du contrat de subvention entre la Commission Européenne et la CEEAC pour l'année 2009.* January 26 2009
    http://www.ceeac-eccas.org/index.php?rubrique=documentation&cat=1&id=240 (accessed September 4, 2009).

19. See: Réseau Francophone de Recherche sur les Opérations de Paix, http://www.operation-spaix.net/MICOPAX (accessed September 10, 2010).

With the transfer of functions from FOMUC to MICOPAX, the mission's responsibilities have been significantly broadened. According to its mandate of 12 July 2008, MICOPAX's mission rests on four pillars. MICOPAX is to assist the CAR government in institutional restructuring, reforming the security sector and in implementing a programme for disarmament, demobilisation and reintegration of ex-combatants (DDR). Moreover, the mission is to help establish and maintain the rule of law and public order and security in the country, and ensure the security of UN staff and the civil population.

As a second objective, MICOPAX is to support the post-conflict political transition in the CAR, notably through the promotion of democratic principles and by supporting the reconciliation and dialogue initiated by the CAR government. MICOPAX is, moreover, to assist with in the preparations for and holding of municipal, parliamentary and presidential elections in 2011.

A third pillar is the mission's responsibility to promote and monitor respect for human rights in the CAR, and a fourth is the coordination of humanitarian aid and participation in the fight against pandemics and endemic diseases, such as AIDS/HIV.[20] MICOPAX's mandate, running from 12 July 2008 and ending by 2013, is to be renewed every six months. It is split into two periods. The first 12 months have been considered a transitional phase, mainly focused on the smooth transfer of authority from CEMAC and ECCAS and on resolving all judicial, financial, logistical and administrative questions. After July 2009, MICOPAX was supposed to fully implement its mandate as a consolidation force.

---

20. CEEAC, *13ème Session Ordinaire de la Conférence des Chefs d'Etats et de Gouvernement ; Décision /CEEAC/CCEG /XlII/08, Portant Mandat de la Mission de Paix du 12 juillet au 31 décembre 2008 et Mission de Consolidation de la Paix du 1er janvier 2009 aux environs de l'année 2013 du Conseil de Paix et de Sécurité de l'Afrique Centrale en République Centrafricaine.* June 12, 2008.

Major Security Challenges in Central Africa

In Central Africa, the so-called "resource curse" thesis is particularly evident (Auty 1993). Although Central Africa is one of Africa's most resource-endowed regions, it is paradoxically made up of the poorest and least-developed countries on the continent. Well endowed with gold, diamonds and uranium, the CAR, for instance, is listed on the penultimate rank of the United Nations Development Programme's Human Development Index (UNDP HDI), with a life expectancy of around 40 to 45 years, 34 per cent of the population having no access to clean water and almost two-thirds of the population living on less than US$ 1.25 a day (UNDP 2009). Whereas the country's poverty can in part be related to the non-exploitation of large parts of its mineral wealth due to the government's limited capacities and fragmented territorial control, a major problem lies in the inefficient use of available resources, the mismanagement of public funds and political and institutional weakness. In this regard, it remains more than questionable whether the recent agreements between the government and the French company AREVA regarding the exploitation of uranium in Bakouma province by 2014–15 will bring any improvemens to the republic's socioeconomic situation.

Central Africa's significant wealth in minerals, oil and timber, together with government failure to access and effectively manage resources, represents a substantial conflict factor. Weak, limited or nonexistent state control over mines and resources makes these resources a potential income source for criminal groups and rebel movements. At the same time, widespread frustration at the state's inability to address basic, social and economic needs, improve well-being and ensure security gives rise to loss of confidence in the public sector and is a key factor in the growing alienation, anger and tensions within a society. In the CAR, the roots of the current insecurity in large parts of the country, especially in the northeast and northwest, can to an extent be traced to the severe political and socioeconomic crisis at the end of the 1990s, when general discontent over growing poverty and the non-payment of salary arrears to civil servants and soldiers culminated in civil unrest and army mutinies.

Among the 10 ECCAS member states, only a few have escaped serious internal crisis and violent conflict during the last two decades. The porosity of national borders, the uncontrolled movement of combatants and armed groups across borders and between different zones of conflict and the proliferation of illegal arms and weapons increase the risk of spill-over from conflicts in neighbouring states. For Debos, this risk is magnified in the case of Chad, Sudan, Uganda and the CAR in particular by the willingness of combatants to readily shift allegiances between conflict parties and rebel movements (Debos 2008).

Apart from the risk of the regionalisation of conflicts and crises, the presence of armed groups is also a direct source of insecurity among the population. In the border provinces of the CAR, the high level of violence by gangs that attack local people and villages, burn down houses, kidnap children for ransom, poach wildlife and rustle cattle has led to the displacement of almost 200,000 Central Africans within the country and a further 150,000 to neighbouring countries, especially Chad (UNHCR 2010).

Finally, an overarching security challenge lies in the internal political in-stability of Central African states. Weak political legitimacy leading to fragile social cohesion threatens the stability of political structures and challenges the capabilities of state institutions. This strengthens centrifugal tendencies, while reducing the reach of governments essentially to capitals and their immediate vicinity. Moreover, in post-conflict settings, the difficulty of reaching arrange-ments and agreements between former conflicting parties impedes the peace process, while the limited willingness of political actors to compromise and build consensus also challenges the "relative" stability in other states. In the CAR, the Inclusive Political Dialogue, launched to foster national reconciliation and settle the year-long crisis, is mainly marked by the political elite's reluctance to share power with the opposition and former opponents and to undertake substantial political reforms.

The "Pros and Cons" Of Regional Peacekeeping in Central Africa

The progressive implementation of peace and security instruments and mechanisms within ECCAS and transfer of authority over the multinational mission have further advanced development of ECCAS from purely economic community to regional framework for security cooperation. In evaluating the global role of regional organisations in conflict management, UN Secretary-General Ban Ki-moon recognised their "growing contribution" to conflict prevention, peacemaking, peacekeeping and peacebuilding. He emphasised that these organisations are "well positioned to understand the root causes of many conflicts and other security challenges close to home and to influence their prevention or resolution, owing to their knowledge of the region."[21]

This statement is in line with the vision stressed by the UN Security Council. In July 2004, Council members underlined the advantages of interventions by regional organisations to enhance peace and security compared to those conducted by the UN.[22] Geographical proximity is likely to result in greater understanding of the threats facing states in the same region and mutual willingness to confront them. Also, in view of the transnational dimension of many conflicts, countries have a shared interest in supporting their neighbours' stability and security. Members of a regional community are also said to share a "homogeneous socio-cultural vision,"[23] while personal relations among political leaders are considered conducive to "fruitful dialogue based on personal trust" (Tavares and Schulz 2006). Finally, regional organisations are considered less bureaucratic and therefore better able to set up a joint mission and to act on the ground promptly, unlike the ponderous decision-making processes of organisations like the UN, which often impede flexible reactions.

Some of the foregoing arguments can to an extent be applied to the case of Central Africa. Without doubt, the agreement in October 2002 by CEMAC states to set up a joint peace mission in Bangui was taken promptly and the progressive deployment of troops began only a few months later. This prompt reaction can certainly also be related to the fact that, except for Gabon, all the countries providing troops to the FOMUC mission between 2002 and 2008 share common borders with the CAR. This fact may have made them more sensitive to the security problems of their neighbour and more concerned about minimising the prospect of escalation and the spill-over of conflict into their own territories.

---

21. United Nations Security Council, 5776th Meeting, November 6, 2007.
22. United Nations Security Council, 5007th Meeting, July 20, 2004. Press Release.
23. United Nations Security Council, 5007th Meeting, July 20, 2004. Press Release.

Critical Constraints in Regional Peace and Security in Central Africa

Funding and insufficient capacities

A major problem facing FOMUC and MICROPAX was the insufficiency of their funding and capacities. During the first months of deployment, FOMUC had only 380 troops, significantly less than the 1,500 combatants supporting Bozizé's coup d'état. FOMUC's strength had increased progressively to 500 armed personnel by July 2008, when it was replaced by MICOPAX. However, the latter's current 527 military personnel may also be insufficient to fulfil the mission's mandate, given the strength of rebel movements in the CAR. The two groups, Union des forces démocratiques pour le rassemblement (UFDR) and Armée populaire pour la restauration de la République et de la démocratie (APRD), are reported to have about 1,000 fighters. Other movements are believed to be operating in the area, such as the Ugandan Lord's Resistance Army, which is estimated to have about 600–700 combatants in the CAR. The Forces démocratiques populaires de Centrafrique (FDPC) is smaller, but is well-equipped and well-armed (Spittaels and Hilgers 2009).

The CAR's national force, Forces armées centrafricaines (FACA), that is supposed to cooperate with the multinational troops, has a relatively small army component as well. Of the 5,000 people on strength, 1,500 are currently operational, the rest being members of the presidential guard (around 1,000 mainly Chadian combatants), military engineers, firefighters and support staff, as well as about 700 inactive, mostly retired soldiers. The strike capacity of FACA troops is further limited by major shortcomings in resources, equipment and training. Moreover, there are frequent problems related to low or late payment (Spittaels and Hilgers 2009).

This weakness in personnel is matched by a lack of resources. Both CEMAC and ECCAS regularly experience severe financial bottlenecks that seriously impede their proper functioning. During FOMUC's deployment, CEMAC had significant financial shortfalls, primarily due to irregular payment of contributions by member states. An assessment undertaken in 2006 revealed that the community's budget could cover the costs of the CEMAC secretariat in Bangui (ECDPM and PMC 2006), but was insufficient for the implementation of community policies and activities. Parts of CEMAC's budget are supposed to be covered by the *Taxe Communautaire d'Intégration* (TCI), specially created to avoid gridlocks similar to those encountered by UDEAC. It is levied by members on imports from outside the CEMAC area and considered a self-financing mechanism for the community. However, the transfer of TCI earnings to the community is often only partial or delayed. In 2002 and 2004, only 19 per cent and 37 per cent respectively of the tax earnings were provided by member states to CEMAC (ECDPM and PMC 2006). This incapacity to cover its budget significantly weakens the effectiveness and performance of the community.

As a result, the FOMUC mission's budget has been covered almost entirely by external donors, primarily by France and after 2004 mainly by the EU and France. Between 2004 and 2008, the EU contributed € 23.4 million to FOMUC's budget,[24] while throughout the mission's deployment, France provided much of the material support as well as contributing to the mission's budget. In contrast, financial contributions by CEMAC member states were marginal. The mission therefore depended completely on external funds (Meyer 2006).

In the case of ECCAS, the situation is similar. The community's regular budget, at about US$ 18 million, is small compared to other African regional communities: ECOWAS's budget is US$ 121 million and SADC's about US$ 45 million (Fanta 2009). Within MICOPAX's budget, international contributions are again significant. In contrast to FOMUC, ECCAS is supposed to provide 20 per cent of the operation's budget, but so far the real contributions by member states have been lower.

This high dependency on external funds is a critical challenge to the idea of African ownership in the case of Central Africa. (Esmenjaud 2009).[25] On one hand, reliance by regional operations on external financial support makes them heavily dependent on budgetary allocations from donor countries and very vulnerable to changes in donor policies. They are thus dependent on the goodwill and continuing commitment of the international community. On the other hand, the central role of external funds within these operations' budgets opens the door to domination by foreign interests. As observed by Cedric de Coning, at the continental level (also in Central Africa states) countries and regional organisations have to comply with the demands and preferences of their "benefactors": "[D]onors can determine the duration of a mission, and can influence a mission's mandate by placing terms and conditions on continued funding, or by withdrawing funding" (de Coning 2002) if they no longer agree with the scope of the mission.

In this regard, the termination in December 2010 of the international MINURCAT peace operation in the border zone between Chad and CAR has

---

24. See also_*"EU relations with the Central African Republic"* published on the Website of the European Commission under: http://ec.europa.eu/development/geographical/regionscountries/countries/country_profile.cfm?cid=cf&type=long&lng=en (accessed June 26, 2008).

25. The concept of African ownership is often used together with the idea of "Africanisation" of conflicts. Whereas the latter refers to the "growing implication of African organisations in conflict management", the idea of "African ownership" is defined as de facto political control over this issue, which requires Africans to exert control over both the ordering of priorities (i.e. the agenda) and the decision-making processes in their institutions. The fulfilment of African ownership is therefore often considered as the precondition for bringing "real African empowerment." See Esmenjaud 2009.

confronted the region with the question of how to fill the security vacuum. Strengthening MICOPAX by increasing troop numbers and widening their deployment to the CAR's border provinces is only possible if supported by international donors. The high level of external dependency not only raises the question of whose interests FOMUC and MICOPAX serve, but also how effective such organisations can be in pursuing the objectives of regional peace and security. It also seems to contradict and be inconsistent with the principles of self-sufficiency, self-reliance and autonomy envisaged by the Lagos Plan of Action as a framework for guiding the regionalisation process in Africa.

Problematic conception of Central Africa as a region

A further, and region-specific challenge to regional peace and security approaches in Central Africa is the difficulty of defining, delimitating and conceiving of Central Africa as a region. First, there is the coexistence of two differently delimited regional communities, with overlapping memberships. Whereas CEMAC comprises only states in the central part of the continent, ECCAS's membership is based on a wider definition, including countries that are part of Southern and Eastern African regional communities, such as Angola, DRC and Burundi. Cameroon, Gabon, CAR, Chad, Republic of the Congo and Equatorial Guinea belong to both CEMAC and ECCAS. As noted above, some states have overlapping memberships in COMESA, EAC, SADC and CEPGL.

This issue is further complicated by the question of the origin of both communities. CEMAC, as we have seen, is the successor to the UDEAC customs union, set up on the basis of the colonially created Federation of French Equatorial Africa (AEF). France's interest in establishing AEF was to ease administration and facilitate economic exchange between its Central African colonies by establishing an institutional framework. Promoting economic cooperation also guided the newly independent states when they agreed to maintain some of these structures and set up a customs union. AEF certainly had an important impact and influence on the future composition of Central Africa as a region and can be seen as one of the principal foundations of CEMAC. However, this external element in CEMAC's history makes it difficult to assume a strong regional consciousness and identity.

The idea behind ECCAS has been overcoming global marginalisation and jointly promoting economic, social and cultural development throughout the continent. Although, it is possible to consider ECCAS as more African-driven than CEMAC, the external influences behind the community's creation are worth noting. Indeed, its creation was very much in response to objectives set by the OAU, not ones primarily agreed at the regional level. A further problem with ECCAS is that it encompasses culturally, socially, economically and politically disparate states: Chad in the Sahel, the Great Lakes countries Burundi and the

DRC, and Southern African Angola. This heterogeneity is compounded by the different historic and linguistic backgrounds of the members, which are former British, French, Spanish as well as Portuguese colonies.

Lack of clear regional leader

In Central Africa, weak regional coherence is further magnified by the absence of a clear regional leader (Awoumou 2008). Unlike in most other regional communities in Africa there is no clear hegemon to promote the interests of the entire region at the internal or the international level, no Nigeria as in West Africa, no South Africa in Southern Africa or Egypt in North Africa. In the case of CEMAC, this role has often been assigned to Cameroon and Gabon as twin leaders (Stevens et al. 2008). In the case of Cameroon, this has been on the basis of its demographic weight and its relative political stability. However, until recently, Cameroon has had only weak aspirations to play a more central role within the region. Gabon is in size and population small but has economic weight as an oil producer, which has made the country a major pole for migration. Its claim to regional leadership mainly rests on late President Omar Bongo's frequent interventions as peacemaker and mediator in conflicts. However, prospects of co-leadership by these two countries have been undermined by the animosities between their presidents. For years, Paul Biya and Omar Bongo avoided each other and never attended the same regional meetings, thereby complicating regional decision-making. Whereas Ali Bongo does not share his father's aspirations to regional leadership), some scope exists for Cameroon to play a more prominent position, at least at the economic level.

Other countries, such as Equatorial Guinea and Chad, have both made claims to regional leadership. Chad's aspiration is often explained by its rise as an oil producer and exporter from 2003. It is reported that "Idriss Déby is setting himself up as the 'boss' of Central Africa. He already has the military power and with the oil he's now got the economic power" (Eriksson and Hagströmer 2005).[26]

Ten times smaller than Gabon and with a population of slightly more than 600,000, Equatorial Guinea justifies its claims to leadership on the basis of its strategic position in the Gulf of Guinea, as well as its new economic status as oil-producing country. To lend these demands more weight, President Obiang Nguema has recently promoted the idea of substantial reform of CEMAC by arguing for greater equity in assigning positions and the principle of rotating among member states the chairs of the main community institutions such as the Bank of Central African States or the Central African States Development

---

26. Statement made by a high-ranking official from one of the six CEMAC countries, cited in Eriksson and Hagströmer 2005: 36.

Bank. The notion of the smallest member of CEMAC and ECCAS being the engine of regional cooperation may seem questionable to the region's heavyweights, such as the DRC or Angola

Analogous to the twin leadership of Cameroon and Gabon within CEMAC, some observers see Kinshasa-Luanda-Yaoundé as the leading axis in ECCAS. The DRC, indeed, has repeatedly claimed the role of regional power. As far back as 1968, for instance, then Zaire took advantage of a disagreement among the UDEAC members to convince Chad and the CAR to quit the community and jointly form the United States of Central Africa. Although this enterprise failed when the CAR and Chad withdrew from the new union, it nevertheless indicates Kinshasa's early aspirations to regional leadership. Today, however, its credibility as a Central African power largely depends on its capacity to settle the crisis on its territory and to promote economic and social development. It remains, moreover, questionable whether Central African states would favour regional leadership by the DRC.

Angola's role as leading nation is constrained largely by the effects of prolonged civil war and the heavy demands of post-conflict reconstruction. Although the country's economic potential, based on oil and diamonds, would certainly qualify it for regional leadership, its position is significantly weakened by the domestic challenges of social and economic reconstruction, the presence of internally displaced people and the reintegration of former combatants. Moreover, Luanda maintains important ties with SADC, a more dynamic regional economic community.

The lack of a clear regional leader is further complicated by foreign intervention in Central Africa. France, in particular, may fear losing sway in what is often called its "backyard" ("pré carré") (Tull 2005; Touati 2007) with the appearance of a regional leader, especially if this were a non-Francophone country.

Dynamics of individual interests

In view of its problematic conception as a region and the absence of a clear regional leader, Central Africa is prone to the intrusion of individual interests. In fact, over the years, Central African regional cooperation has largely been pervaded by the political or economic interests of ruling elites, which have significantly guided decisions, activities and also regional security missions. As a result, regional peace and security cooperation is increasingly overshadowed by the interplay of political interests within the communities and the influence these interests exert on community tasks and policies (Meyer 2010).

The analysis of FOMUC and MICOPAX underscores how Central African political actors' interests have influenced or even undermined peace operations. Parallels can be readily drawn between these operations' mandates and the specific concerns of political leaders to consolidate their eroded power and sovereignty. FOMUC's initial mission was to protect President Patassé against his opponents. In 2003, after Bozizé's successful coup, the redefinition of the mandate very much met the new regime's interests. The mission thenceforth fought rebel movements and criminals in the north, northeast and northwest of the country seeking to undermine Bozizé's authority.

The question can thus be raised as to how much regional interventions really meet the security needs of the population. Although actions to suppress non-state criminal actors led to some reduction of the violence against the local population, the social, economic and political needs of the people were not directly and sufficiently considered and addressed.

This dominance of political interests is a great challenge to major peacekeeping efforts. The Inclusive Political Dialogue between the main belligerents in the CAR in December 2008 is a recent example. These talks were a broadly welcomed development and widely supported and backed by MICOPAX. They brought together representatives of government and the main rebel movements, and were joined by opposition parties and civil society. However, the promising results of this initiative were seriously compromised by the clash of individual interests and, once again, the predominance of the regime's interests over national ones.[27] Indeed, according to the International Crisis Group (ICG) in January 2010, implementation of major concessions reached during the talks has been largely thwarted by the uncompromising positions of the main parties, notably the government's attempt to use the Dialogue to advance its own power.

As a result, despite modest "laudable efforts" to carry out reform, there was no significant progress in 2009 towards stability and security.[28] On the contrary, the gap between rhetoric and reality has remained wide. Especially the government has been increasingly reluctant to put into practice exactly what was agreed. In January 2009, Bozizé dissolved the old government as recommended, but instead of creating a consensus government, reappointed Faustin-Archange Touadéra as prime minister. This "new" government included 10 of the previous ministers, including Bozizé as defence minister. Representatives of the rebel movements, opposition parties and civil society were given only very symbolic positions. In view of this and government's reluctance to launch further governance reforms, rebel leaders also proved unwilling to follow through with their

---

27. The Inclusive Political Dialogue took place from December 8-20, 2008 in Bangui. The almost 200 participants included representatives of the presidential majority in the national assembly, opposition and non-aligned parties, the civil service and of civil society, as well as members from APRD, UFDR, MLCJ (Mouvement des Libérateurs Centrafricains pour la Justice/Movement of Central African Liberators for Justice) and UFR (Union des Forces Républicaines/Union of Republican Forces).

28. Transcript of the follow-up committee president's press conference, annex to its evaluation report, June 2009, cit. in International Crisis Group (ICG) 2010: 7.

concessions. According to the ICG assessment, a major interest of the president in holding the Dialogue was to prove his goodwill and political openness to the international donor community and thereby "boost his credibility as a statesman" (ICG 2010: 3). It remains, however, questionable that the country's security has been improved in a sustainable and stable manner.

Other governments have also attempted to use CEMAC and ECCAS for their own political interests. Chad's contribution to the FOMUC mission may indeed appear rather dubious in view of the very strained relations between President Patassé and his Chadian counterpart, Idriss Déby, during 2002. Both leaders accused each other of backing rebel movements in their respective countries. Serious doubts are raised about the neutrality and impartiality of FOMUC by the reported support in arms and troops – the so-called Libérateurs – that François Bozizé received from the Chadian government in the coup that toppled Patassé in 2003 (ICG 2007).

According to ICG, an even larger collaboration among CEMAC states lay behind Bozizé's coup, with logistical, financial or at least political support coming from the DRC, Republic of the Congo and Gabon, as well as Chad. FOMUC troops would have received clear orders not to intervene against Bozizé, which largely explains their inactivity during the putsch.[29] Patassé had supported Jean-Pierre Bemba's rebellion in DRC, so the end of his regime put more pressure on Bemba to accept the DRC government's power-sharing agreements (Stevens et al. 2008: 170).

The quests for regional leadership outlined earlier can also be understood as being strongly influenced and guided by political actors' individual interests and not necessarily those of the community. According to Eriksson and Hagströmer, Déby's regional ambitions, for instance, correlated with his efforts to protect the oilfields on Chadian territory from any force that might endanger his control of them. Déby reportedly played a key role in several military coups, such as those in the Republic of the Congo (1997), DRC (1998) and in CAR (2002, 2003). Although the Chadian president always denied these accusations, the regime changes in these countries very much served to consolidate his control over oil revenues and in the assertion of his power over Chad.

In sum, the central problem for Central African regionalisation and peace and security cooperation in particular is the lack of commitment by states and their leaders to promoting a common long-term vision. In principle, Central African states favour regional cooperation because of the mutual economic and political advantages it is supposed to provide (Stevens at al. 2008). However, in view of their own weakness and limited resources, governments tend to support

---

29. The report refers to an interview with a high-ranking officer, who explained that only the Congolese contingent did not receive these orders in time. Therefore, it was the only FOMUC contingent to intervene against Bozizé's movement. (ICG 2007:16 (footnote 81).

those joint activities that bring direct and short-term benefits for them. Regional initiatives and instruments thus fall easy prey to political manipulation often not in line with the objectives of the community or other members.

Consequently, CEMAC's and ECCAS's regional peace and security initiatives seem to privilege short-term actions that largely focus on protecting political regimes and facilitating external hegemonic designs by reacting to military threats, such as rebellions or coups d'état, or settling armed conflicts between or within member states. A long-term approach towards self-sustaining security that also considers the needs and human security concerns of Central African peoples seems to be plagued by a host of problems, not least the commitment of the region's political leaders. This shortcoming is likely to hamper growth and development throughout the region, while fostering conditions conducive to continued insecurity and instability.

Prospects for Enhanced Regional Peace and Security Cooperation in Central Africa

The problem of intergovernmental cooperation

From the beginning, regional cooperation in Central Africa has followed an intergovernmental approach. CEMAC and ECCAS are organised along inter-governmental lines, as was UDEAC before them. They are primarily focused on promoting cooperation, agreement and understanding between member states, who are the prime actors and whose direct representatives at the regional level have the main decision-making power. So far, the transfer of sovereignty from the states to the regional level has been insignificant. Consequently, in both instances the main regional institutions – the secretariats, CEMAC's court of justice and the parliaments – are weak. They have mainly advisory functions and support and implement decisions by the heads of state. The problem with this form of institutional organisation is that it has marginal potential for re-sponding to the above insecurity concerns in Central Africa and contributing to state stability.

As wars, in general, most often occur within proximate states, increased co-operation and establishing common institutions and agreements can contribute to preventing interstate friction and crises. According to classical regionalisation theories, notably those prevailing during the Cold War, regional state alliances as instrumental to fostering international peace and security.[30]

In the case of Central Africa, however, the risk of conflicts between states is largely outweighed by rising insecurity within states. Hence, the main thrust of regional cooperation to improve security should not lie in reducing the risk of international conflicts between member states. More important is that coopera-tion which contributes to better addressing factors that challenge and under-mine transnational security and stability. If regional cooperation is to contribute to regional peace and security in Central Africa, this is unlikely to be through its potential to attenuate and regulate the military and political power of states. Much more important is the capacity to transcend the weakness of states as security providers and in meeting the human security needs of citizens. This, however, speaks in favour of further deepening regional cooperation in Central Africa and especially giving greater emphasis to a more supranational people-

---

30. For Realist and Neo-Realist theories, see: Kenneth N. Waltz, *Theory of International Politics*, Reading MA: Addison-Wesley, 1979, and Stephen Walt, *The Origins of Alliances*, Ithaca NY: Cornell University Press, 1987. For Functionalism, see: Robert O. Keohane, *International Institutions and State Power: Essays in International Relations Theory*, Boulder/San Francisco, London: Westview, 1989; and Andrew Moravcsik, "Taking Preferences Seriously. A Liberal Theory of International Politics", *International Organisations*, Fall 1997, vol. 51, no. 4, 513–53 For discussion on the different impacts of regional cooperation on peace and security, see also Angela Meyer, 2006.

oriented approach to regional integration instead of the current form of inter-governmental and state-driven cooperation.

The security relevance of supranational integration

The concept of regional integration extends beyond the idea of intergovernmental cooperation, beyond alliances between sovereign actors and reduction of co-operation to agreements and conventions. The more and deeper integration is pursued, the more it leads to limitation of state sovereignty or – more precisely – a different way of exercising sovereignty in common.[31]

Especially the European integration process has attracted much theoretical interest and largely placed in question the relevance of more classical Cold-War influenced theories (Giering 1997, De Lombaerde and Van Langenhove 2007). As with intergovernmental cooperation, supranational integration is also a fa-vourable foundation for consolidating peace among concerned states. As the case of Europe shows, concerted policy-making and common policies in ever more sectors increases interdependence and limits the scope for interstate conflicts.

Moreover, integration has significant potential for promoting security and stability within states. This is especially true when security is defined more com-prehensively, going beyond purely military aspects to include the often non-military roots of conflicts and crises. As many sociopolitical, economic or en-vironmental threats are large scale, transnational or ubiquitous, they require solutions beyond a purely national scope. Indeed, single-state approaches often prove insufficient, inefficient or not far-reaching enough.

Similarly, regional integration can strengthen weak state legitimacy. As the CAR case shows, a major breeding ground for Central African crises and insta-bility is, in part, the loss of public confidence in the state as security provider. When the state and ruling elites fail to satisfy the population's security require-ments and basic needs, state authorities widely lose their credibility. If, on the other hand, joint policies and activities at the regional level result in solving issues not properly addressed on the national level, this successful delivery of policies and services can build a new basis for legitimacy (Meyer 2008).

Realising this potential is, however, linked to several conditions. In par-ticular, it requires empowerment of inclusive national democratic institutions and processes, supranational structures and institutional mechanisms and an increase in their competences. Without sufficient power to control and coor-dinate their members, regional institutions will have little ability to increase accountability, transparency and efficiency. As long as member accountability

---

31. See also: Contribution of Adrian Severin, MP (Romania), alternate member to the Euro-pean Convention: The Missions of Europe, in: Convention Bulletin Edition 06 - 03.05.02, available on: http://www.constitutional-convention.net/bulletin/archives/000083.html (ac-cessed January 23, 2010).

remains limited, regional institutions will not be able to monitor and control effective implementation of regional policies and to reduce the scope for political leaders to prioritise individual over collective interests. They also remain helpless against mismanagement and corruption.

Another central element is stronger involvement by non-state actors in the regionalisation process. In particular, participation by civil society actors can counterbalance the state-centric and interest-driven approach characteristic of intergovernmental cooperation. This is indeed essential for increasing the emphasis on human security needs.

Strengthening the supranational level

Although the institutional architecture of CEMAC and ECCAS has formally been widened to include a parliament and court of justice, the effective level of supranational control nevertheless remains low and underdeveloped. In the case of ECCAS, the establishment of the network of parliamentarians is still incomplete, while the creation of CEMAC's parliament has regularly been delayed. In August 2010, the parliament was finally inaugurated in Malabo. The deputies' powers to influence developments are, however, restricted. Instead, the parliament's role is limited to representation and advisory functions. Similarly, CEMAC's court of justice has little enforcement power: the judges can point out violations of community law but have no power to impose sanctions (Meyer 2009). Consequently, member state accountability remains limited.

By contrast, in other African regional communities, specific supranational approaches have been established to address lack of commitment by member states. SADC, for instance, is very strict about member states that fail to meet their commitments. In 2003, Seychelles was deprived of the right to participate in community meetings and finally quit the organisation a year later after it did not pay its contributions on time. Although CEMAC and ECCAS have similar directives, they have never been enforced, despite significant payment arrears. Indeed, exclusion of defaulting members requires the unanimous assent of other – also not-so-dutiful – member states. Thus, the powers of CEMAS and ECCAS remain negligible on this point.

Adopting a multi-actor approach

In regard to the need to further involve non-state actors in regionalisation initiatives, some other regional processes in Africa have made significant progress over the past 10 years by increasingly adopting a multi-actor approach. Civil society tends to be involved in agenda-setting processes through specific channels. In Western and Southern Africa, representatives from civil society organisations have organised specific forums. The West African Civil Society Forum (WAC-SOF) and the Council of Non Governmental Organisations (SADC-CNGO) meet prior to the respective ECOWAS and SADC heads of state summits to give statements and elaborate recommendations. WACSOF also audits the implementation of regional policies at the national level and advocates on behalf of human security and other concerns within their region.

By comparison, a multi-actor approach has been neglected in Central Africa. CEMAC and ECCAS both remain largely state-driven. The role of non-state actors in decision-making, agenda-setting and policy implementation processes is still undeveloped and marginal. Civil society in particular plays no significant role in stimulating, participating in or interacting with the regionalisation process.

This circumstance can certainly be related to problems and weaknesses in the civil society. Compared to other regions in Africa, notably Southern and Western Africa, the development of civil societies and civil society organisations is relatively recent in Central Africa. In a number of states, this process has been further complicated and handicapped since the mid- 1990s by social and political tensions. Most local civil society organisations face funding and capacity problems and seldom cooperate or network with a view to pooling available resources and augmenting their weight and importance. At the same time, in Central Africa relations between civil society and governments are often rather problematic, as political leaders may perceive civil society organisations as troublemakers and opponents. The main advantage of civil society organisations lies in their proximity to the people and the knowledge of their needs, concerns and interests, allowing them a bridging role as mediator and community mouthpiece.[32]

In CEMAC, the potential role of civil society has been only marginally acknowledged. In the case of ECCAS, one can discern some first indicators of a slow but progressive opening up of the regionalisation process to civil society. Indeed, the role of the civil society in conflict management and peacekeeping is being increasingly recognised as part of ECCAS's regional activities. With the support of the EC's PAPS, ECCAS launched a comprehensive programme in September 2007 to improve cooperation with civil society groups in Central Africa. This decision was largely based on growing acknowledgement of the centrality of these non-state actors' contributions to the prevention and resolution of conflicts. In the words of the ECCAS secretary-general, "[t]oday, national security cannot be reserved for experts. It concerns all of us, as it is not only about ensuring state security but also the human security of populations. It is therefore

---

32. On the role of the civil society, see also: The Center for Conflict Resolution, *The Peacebuilding Role of Civil Society in Central Africa*. Policy Seminar Report, Douala, Cameroon, 2006.

natural that all are associated with the discussion about priorities and means."[33] To foster interaction between ECCAS and Central African civil society, selected civil society organisations have taken part in training and workshops on security issues. Civil society representatives have also helped monitor elections, such as in Angola in September 2008.

A further example of the progressively growing role of civil society in ECCAS security cooperation is the *Programme de Renforcement des Capacités et Gestion des Conflits de la Société Civile en Afrique Centrale* (Capacity building project for civil society organisations for conflict prevention and management in Central Africa (PREGESCO).[34] PREGESCO is a joint project launched by civil society organisations in eight ECCAS states.[35] It is coordinated by the Congolese NGO *Service de Renforcement des Appuis aux Communautés de base en Afrique Centrale*, based in Kinshasa. PREGESCO's members are regular invitees to the meetings of some of ECCAS's institutions. In June 2009, they participated in the activities of the ECCAS consultative commission in Kinshasa. PREGESCO is also regularly accredited to provide observers, alongside those from ECCAS and the AU, to monitor elections in Central African states and elsewhere on the continent. Finally, PREGESCO also participates in studies carried out by ECCAS, such as that on transborder relations in December 2008, and organises joint multi-stakeholder seminars and workshops at the regional level, for instance on security sector reform and early warning.

The potential of this development to contribute to a more integrative approach to regionalisation, especially the consolidation of peace and security in Central Africa, is intrinsically linked to three conditions. First, if regional cooperation is to meet the population's basic needs by promoting a climate of security and stability, it needs to ensure that the multi-actor approach addresses both large-scale civil society organisations and smaller ones. Larger organisations are most often located in capitals or major cities, and lack direct contact with local rural populations. Smaller organisations may have better connections on the ground and usually have a better knowledge of the security needs and concerns in specific provinces, knowledge essential in conceiving of policies or for the early detection of security threats and risks. However, for resource and capacity

---

33. Translation by the author: "Aujourd'hui, la sécurité nationale ne peut être réservée aux experts. Elle est l'affaire de tous, puisqu'il s'agit non seulement d'assurer la sécurité de l'Etat, mais aussi la sécurité humaine des populations. Il est donc naturel que tous soient associés à la discussion de ses priorités et de ses moyens." Discours d'ouverture du Secrétaire Général au séminaire sous régional sur la réforme des secteurs de la sécurité, January 14, 2009, available on the website of ECCAS :http://www.ceeac-eccas.org/index.php?rubrique=documentation&cat=6&id=230 (accessed July 26, 2009).
34. See also PREGESCO's website: www.pregesco.org (accessed July 26, 2009).
35. Burundi, Cameroon, the Republic of the Congo, Gabon, the CAR, the DRC, Rwanda and Chad.

reasons, smaller organisations may have difficulty in acting on the community level. A solution may lie in ensuring the connection between large and small civil society organisations and encouraging the constant exchange of information. Or, alternatively, a suitable model may be setting up forums that represent civil society interests, similar to WACSOF and SADC-CNGO.

A second, closely related precondition is the availability of organisational and resource capacities. If civil society organisations are to represent local interests at the community level, they need support. PREGESCO, for instance, operates national offices, in addition to its headquarters in Kinshasa, to ensure that its project members know the ground. However, as the project's report of 2008 pointed out, this decentralised structure is largely constrained by a constant lack of resources and capacities.[36] The project is only covered by the African Capacity Building Fund, whereas facilities in Kinshasa are provided by the DRC government. No funding comes from ECCAS or the other member states.

Third, it is important that a multi-actor approach to regional security and stability have a clear role and place for civil society actors to contribute to the implementation and elaboration of regional community security actions and policies in order to give more emphasis to local needs and concerns. Given the current intergovernmental nature of CEMAC and ECCAS, the inclusion of civil society in regional decision-making would imply institutional change and progress. Here, however, the major challenge remains the unwillingness of state leaders to commit themselves to a transformative agenda for regional cooperation, peace and security.

---

36. See the report available on www.pregesco.org (accessed July 26, 2009).

Conclusion

Insecurity and instability in Central Africa are intrinsically linked to the weakness of states as sovereign powers and the limited ability of state structures to maintain social and political order and ensure territorial integrity. A major challenge to regional peace and security relates to the issue of political commitment by the leadership of member states. Because state leaders recognise that their ability to exert state power is limited by weak institutional structures, capacities and infrastructure as well by the existence and subversive activities of non-state political forces, their willingness to cede sovereignty to the community level has remained low.

In the absence of a common vision or "regional consciousness", regional politics is further undermined by individual interests and the failure to further deepen the regionalisation process. Thus, community activities tend to be increasingly used by political actors to demonstrate their role as legitimate rulers of sovereign states and to further defend their political interests. The way in which community summits and conferences are celebrated, as well as the quarrels over the location of headquarters and distribution of posts in regional bodies and institutions, indeed raises the question whether these events and institutions are not used by national elites to enhance their prestige and demonstrate their political importance rather than for promoting agreements and regional policies. This doubt is strengthened by the fact that a significant number of jointly taken decisions remain on paper or are only partly, slowly or belatedly implemented.

Current community-level responses, such as the deployment of FOMUC and MICOPAX and the setting up of the Central African peace and security architecture, indicate that such actions tend first of all to address the symptoms of insecurity and instability, but largely neglect their roots and underlying causes. They do not sufficiently consider the non-military elements of insecurity, such as structural problems that often are at the base of riots, rebellions and violence.

Moving beyond the current intergovernmental structures of CEMAC and ECCAS and deepening regional integration could be a viable option for increasing the security potential of regional cooperation in Central Africa. Indeed, strengthening the supranational level and increasing civil society actor participation in regional decision-making could counterbalance the interest-driven nature of regionalisation, and lead to the better handling of underlying interests and greater emphasis on addressing human security needs and concerns.

The international community should provide more incentives for deepening and strengthening regional cooperation and integration. By further favouring bi-regional over bilateral relations, especially the EU should facilitate consolidation of regional entities, such as CEMAC and ECCAS (Meyer 2010). Such a trend has in fact been under way since 2000 and has been confirmed by the Africa-EU

Strategic Partnership in 2007, as well as by the creation of the Economic Partnership Agreements. On the one hand, European emphasis on African regional communities as partners can be an important incentive for the Central African regionalisation process. It could encourage Central African political leaders to consider CEMAC and ECCAS as significant political, economic and security actors. In addition, intensification of bi-regional relations could improve the relationship between Europe and the Central African region. Whereas today, these relations are largely driven by national interests, including on the European side, these interests could be better and more constructively aligned if more emphasis is given to increasingly coordinated inter-regional dialogue.

It is, however, essential that the international community only support and encourage progress by regional processes towards more democratic and effective forms of integration that give primacy to development and human security, by always respecting the principle of own responsibility and mutual benefit. Under such conditions, further developing and exploiting the potential of regional cooperation to promote self-sustaining peace and security in Central Africa may be possible.

Bibliography

African Union (AU)/Peace and Security Council, 2008, Report of the Chairperson of the Commission on the Situation in the Central African Republic (CAR) 130th meeting, Addis Ababa, May 29.

Auty, R.M., 1993, *Sustaining Development in Mineral Economies. The Resource Curse Thesis*. London: Routledge.

Awoumou, C.D.G., 2008, 'ECCAS or CEMAC. Which Regional Economic Community For Central Africa?', in Chrysantus Ayangafac (ed.), *Political Economy of Regionalisation in Central Africa,* ISS Monograph Series No. 155.

Balencie, J-M. and A. de la Grange, 2001, *Mondes Rebelles. Guérillas, milices, groupes terroristes*. Paris: Michalon.

Binoua, B., 2005, *Centrafrique: l'instabilité permanente.* Paris: Harmattan.

Debos, M., 2008, 'Fluid Loyalties in a Regional Crisis: Chadian "Ex-liberators" in the Central African Republic', *African Affairs*, No. 427:225–241.

de Coning, C., 2002, 'Peacekeeping in Africa: The Next Decade', *Conflict Trends*, No. 3, 55.

De Lombaerde, P. and L. Van Langenhove, 2007, 'Regional Integration, Poverty and Social Policy', *Global Social Policy* 7(3):377-83.

Economic Community of Central African States (ECCAS) (2010), Communication du Général Louis Sylvain-Goma, Secrétaire Général de la CEEAC, à l'occasion de la 'Journée de la Paix et de la Sécurité en Afrique : Décision des Chefs d'Etat et de Gouvernement de l'Union Africaine', September 21.

Eriksson, H. and B. Hagströmer, 2005, *Chad – Towards Democratisation or Petro-Dictatorship?* Discussion Paper 29. Uppsala: Nordiska Afrikainstitutet.

Esmenjaud, R., 2009, 'Peace and security, external actors and the African Union: Africanisation without African ownership', Paper presented at the ECAS Conference 2009, Leipzig, June 4-7.

European Centre for Development Policy Management (ECDPM) and Performances Management Consulting (PMC) (2006), Diagnostic institutionnel, fonctionnel et organisationnel de la CEMAC. Tome I. *Rapport Final* (Assessment Report on CEMAC).

Faes, G. and S. Smith, 2000, 'République centrafricaine : La solitude et le Chaos', *Politique Internationale* 88:281-96.

Fanta, E., 2009, 'The Capacity of African Regional Organisations in Peace and Security', Paper presented at the ERD Workshop: Transforming Political Structures, Instruments and Regional Integration Mechanisms, Florence, April 16-17.

Giering, C., 1997, Europa zwischen Zweckverband und Superstaat. Die Entwicklung der politikwissenschaftlichen Integrationstheorie im Prozess der europäischen Integration, Bonn: Europa Union Verlag (Münchner Beiträge zur Europäischen Einigung, Bd. 1).

Glaser, A. and S. Smith, 2006, *Comment la France a perdu l'Afrique*. Paris: Hachette.

Gounin, Y., 2009, *La France en Afrique. Le combat des Anciens et des Modernes*. Brussels: Debroeck.

Harélimana, J-B., 2008, 'La commission de consolidation de la paix en République centrafricaine : vers un nouveau chapitre de paix', Multipol, December 20, http://www.multipol.org (accessed October 19, 2010).

International Crisis Group (ICG), 2007, 'République Centrafricaine. Anatomie d'un Etat fantôme', *Rapport Afrique*, No.136.

—, 2010, 'Central African Republic: Keeping the Dialogue Alive', Crisis Group *Africa Briefing* No. 69.

Jean, M., 2008, 'Le chemin de l'Occident. Le Blanc en Afrique : de la colonisation à l'aide internationale', online publication http://www.tiersmonde.net/IMG/pdf/L_essai_2__2_.pdf (accessed Octobre 19, 2010)

Kurth, J., 2005, 'Humanitarian Intervention After Iraq: Legal Ideals vs. Military Realities', *Orbis* (Winter): 87–101.

Marchesin, P., 1998, 'La politique africaine de la France en transition', *Politique africaine*, No. 71:91–106

Mehler, A., 2001, 'Zentralafrikanische Republik', in Hofmeier, R. and A. Mehler (ed.), *Afrika Jahrbuch 2000*. Opladen: Leske + Budrich Verlag: 219–23.

—, 2008, 'Positive, ambiguous or negative Peacekeeping in the local security fabric', *Critical Currents* 5:41–65.

Meyer, A., 2006, 'L'intégration régionale et son influence sur la structure, la sécurité et la stabilité d'Etats faibles. L'exemple de quatre Etats centrafricains.' Institut d'Etudes Politiques de Paris (thèse de doctorat).

—, 2008, 'Regional Integration and Security in Central Africa – Assessment and Perspectives 10 years after the revival', Egmont Paper No. 25 http://www.egmontinstitute.be/paperegm/ep25.pdf (accessed April 25, 2009).

—, 2009, 'The democratization of the Central African Economic and Monetary Community (CEMAC)', contribution to the project "International Democracy Watch" (publication forthcoming).

—, 2010, 'Regional Conflict Management in Central Africa: From FOMUC to MICOPAX', in Söderbaum, F. and R. Tavares (eds), *Regional Organizations in African Security*. Routledge: London: 90–106.

Obi, C.I., 2010, 'Economic Community of West African States on the Ground: Comparing Peacekeeping in Liberia, Sierra Leone, Guinea Bissau, and Côte D'Ivoire', in Söderbaum, F. and R. Tavares (eds), *Regional Organizations in African Security*. Routledge: London: 51–67.

Schleicher, H-G., 2004, 'Regionale Sicherheitsbemühungen im südlichen Afrika am Beispiel der SADC', Verband für internationale Politik und Völkerrecht, Vortragsreihe, Berlin.

Schoeman, M. and M. Muller, 2010, 'Southern African Development Community as Regional Peacekeeper: Myth or Reality', in Söderbaum, F. and R. Tavares (eds), *Regional Organizations in African Security*. Routledge: London: 107–24.

Spittaels, S. and F. Hilgert, 2009, *Mapping Conflict Motives: The Central African Republic.* Antwerp: International Peace Information Service.

Stevens, S., H. Hoebeke and K. Vlassenroot, 2008, 'Politics of regional integration in Central Africa, in Chrysantus Ayangafac (ed.), *Political Economy of Regionalisation in Central Africa.* ISS Monograph Series No 155:165–86.

Tavares, R. and M. Schulz, 2006, 'Measuring the Impact of Regional Organisations on Peace Building', in Philippe de Lombaerde (ed.), *Assessment and Measurement of Regional Integration.* London: Routledge.

Touati, S., 2007, 'French Foreign Policy in Africa: Between Pré Carré and Multilateralism', *An Africa Programme Briefing Note*, Chatham House.

Tull, D., 2005, 'France's Africa Policy at a Turning Point', SWP Comments 45.

United Nations Development Programme (UNDP), 2009, *The Human Development Report* 2009. New York.

United Nations High Commissioner for Refugees (UNHCR), 2009, *Global Appeal* 2010–2011.

DISCUSSION PAPERS PUBLISHED BY THE INSTITUTE

Recent issues in the series are available electronically for download free of charge
www.nai.uu.se

1. Kenneth Hermele and Bertil Odén, *Sanctions and Dilemmas. Some Implications of Economic Sanctions against South Africa.* 1988. 43 pp. ISBN 91-7106-286-6

2. Elling Njål Tjönneland, *Pax Pretoriana. The Fall of Apartheid and the Politics of Regional Destabilisation.* 1989. 31 pp. ISBN 91-7106-292-0

3. Hans Gustafsson, Bertil Odén and Andreas Tegen, *South African Minerals. An Analysis of Western Dependence.* 1990. 47 pp. ISBN 91-7106-307-2

4. Bertil Egerö, *South African Bantustans. From Dumping Grounds to Battlefronts.* 1991. 46 pp. ISBN 91-7106-315-3

5. Carlos Lopes, *Enough is Enough! For an Alternative Diagnosis of the African Crisis.* 1994. 38 pp. ISBN 91-7106-347-1

6. Annika Dahlberg, *Contesting Views and Changing Paradigms.* 1994. 59 pp. ISBN 91-7106-357-9

7. Bertil Odén, *Southern African Futures. Critical Factors for Regional Development in Southern Africa.* 1996. 35 pp. ISBN 91-7106-392-7

8. Colin Leys and Mahmood Mamdani, *Crisis and Reconstruction – African Perspectives.* 1997. 26 pp. ISBN 91-7106-417-6

9. Gudrun Dahl, *Responsibility and Partnership in Swedish Aid Discourse.* 2001. 30 pp. ISBN 91-7106-473-7

10. Henning Melber and Christopher Saunders, *Transition in Southern Africa – Comparative Aspects.* 2001. 28 pp. ISBN 91-7106-480-X

11. *Regionalism and Regional Integration in Africa.* 2001. 74 pp. ISBN 91-7106-484-2

12. Souleymane Bachir Diagne, et al., *Identity and Beyond: Rethinking Africanity.* 2001. 33 pp. ISBN 91-7106-487-7

13. Georges Nzongola-Ntalaja, et al., *Africa in the New Millennium.* Edited by Raymond Suttner. 2001. 53 pp. ISBN 91-7106-488-5

14. *Zimbabwe's Presidential Elections 2002.* Edited by Henning Melber. 2002. 88 pp. ISBN 91-7106-490-7

15. Birgit Brock-Utne, *Language, Education and Democracy in Africa.* 2002. 47 pp. ISBN 91-7106-491-5

16. Henning Melber et al., *The New Partnership for Africa's development (NEPAD).* 2002. 36 pp. ISBN 91-7106-492-3

17. Juma Okuku, *Ethnicity, State Power and the Democratisation Process in Uganda.* 2002. 42 pp. ISBN 91-7106-493-1

18. Yul Derek Davids, et al., *Measuring Democracy and Human Rights in Southern Africa.* Compiled by Henning Melber. 2002. 50 pp. ISBN 91-7106-497-4

19. Michael Neocosmos, Raymond Suttner and Ian Taylor, *Political Cultures in Democratic South Africa.* Compiled by Henning Melber. 2002. 52 pp. ISBN 91-7106-498-2

20. Martin Legassick, *Armed Struggle and Democracy. The Case of South Africa.* 2002. 53 pp. ISBN 91-7106-504-0

21. Reinhart Kössler, Henning Melber and Per Strand, *Development from Below. A Namibian Case Study.* 2003. 32 pp. ISBN 91-7106-507-5

22. Fred Hendricks, *Fault-Lines in South African Democracy. Continuing Crises of Inequality and Injustice.* 2003. 32 pp. ISBN 91-7106-508-3

23. Kenneth Good, *Bushmen and Diamonds. (Un) Civil Society in Botswana.* 2003. 39 pp. ISBN 91-7106-520-2

24. Robert Kappel, Andreas Mehler, Henning Melber and Anders Danielson, *Structural Stability in an African Context.* 2003. 55 pp. ISBN 91-7106-521-0

25. Patrick Bond, *South Africa and Global Apartheid. Continental and International Policies and Politics.* 2004. 45 pp. ISBN 91-7106-523-7

26. Bonnie Campbell (ed.), *Regulating Mining in Africa. For whose benefit?* 2004. 89 pp. ISBN 91-7106-527-X

27. Suzanne Dansereau and Mario Zamponi, *Zimbabwe – The Political Economy of Decline.* Compiled by Henning Melber. 2005. 43 pp. ISBN 91-7106-541-5

28. Lars Buur and Helene Maria Kyed, *State Recogni-tion of Traditional Authority in Mozambique. The nexus of Community Representation and State Assist-ance.*
2005. 30 pp. ISBN 91-7106-547-4

29. Hans Eriksson and Björn Hagströmer, *Chad – Towards Democratisation or Petro-Dictatorship?*
2005. 82 pp.ISBN 91-7106-549-

30. Mai Palmberg and Ranka Primorac (eds), *Skinning the Skunk – Facing Zimbabwean Futures.*
2005. 40 pp. ISBN 91-7106-552-0

31. Michael Brüntrup, Henning Melber and Ian Taylor, *Africa, Regional Cooperation and the World Market – Socio-Economic Strategies in Times of Global Trade Regimes.* Com-piled by Henning Melber.
2006. 70 pp. ISBN 91-7106-559-8

32. Fibian Kavulani Lukalo, *Extended Handshake or Wrestling Match? – Youth and Urban Culture Celebrating Politics in Kenya.*
2006.58 pp. ISBN 91-7106-567-9

33. Tekeste Negash, *Education in Ethiopia: From Crisis to the Brink of Collapse.*
2006. 55 pp. ISBN 91-7106-576-8

34. Fredrik Söderbaum and Ian Taylor (eds) *Micro-Regionalism in West Africa. Evidence from Two Case Studies.*
2006. 32 pp. ISBN 91-7106-584-9

35. Henning Melber (ed.), *On Africa – Scholars and African Studies.*
2006. 68 pp. ISBN 978-91-7106-585-8

36. Amadu Sesay, *Does One Size Fit All? The Sierra Leone Truth and Reconciliation Commission Revisited.*
2007. 56 pp. ISBN 978-91-7106-586-5

37. Karolina Hulterström, Amin Y. Kamete and Henning Melber, *Political Opposition in African Countries – The Case of Kenya, Namibia, Zambia and Zimbabwe.*
2007. 86 pp. ISBN 978-7106-587-2

38. Henning Melber (ed.), *Governance and State Delivery in Southern Africa. Examples from Botswana, Namibia and Zimbabwe.*
2007. 65 pp. ISBN 978-91-7106-587-2

39. Cyril Obi (ed.), *Perspectives on Côte d'Ivoire: Between Political Breakdown and Post-Conflict Peace.*
2007. 66 pp. ISBN 978-91-7106-606-6

40. Anna Chitando, *Imagining a Peaceful Society. A Vision of Children's Literature in a Post-Conflict Zimbabwe.*
2008. 26 pp. ISBN 978-91-7106-623-7

41. Olawale Ismail, *The Dynamics of Post-Conflict Reconstruction and Peace Building in West Africa. Between Change and Stability.*
2009.52 pp. ISBN 978-91-7106-637-4

42. Ron Sandrey and Hannah Edinger, *Examining the South Africa–China Agricultural Relationship.*
2009. 58 pp. ISBN 978-91-7106-643-5

43. Xuan Gao, *The Proliferation of Anti-Dumping and Poor Governance in Emerging Economies.*
2009. 41 pp. ISBN 978-91-7106-644-2

44. Lawal Mohammed Marafa, *Africa's Business and Development Relationship with China. Seeking Moral and Capital Values of the Last Economic Frontier.*
2009. xx pp. ISBN 978-91-7106-645-9

45. Mwangi wa Githinji, *Is That a Dragon or an Elephant on Your Ladder? The Potential Impact of China and India on Export Led Growth in African Countries.*
2009. 40 pp. ISBN 978-91-7106-646-6

46. Jo-Ansie van Wyk, *Cadres, Capitalists, Elites and Coalitions. The ANC, Business and Development in South Africa.*
2009. 61 pp. ISBN 978-91-7106-656-5

47. Elias Courson, *Movement for the Emancipation of the Niger Delta (MEND). Political Marginalization, Repression and Petro-Insurgency in the Niger Delta.*2009. 30 pp. ISBN 978-91-7106-657-2

48. Babatunde Ahonsi, *Gender Violence and HIV/AIDS in Post-Conflict West Africa. Issues and Responses.* 2010.
38 pp. ISBN 978-91-7106-665-7

49. Usman Tar and Abba Gana Shettima, *Endangered Democracy? The Struggle over Secularism and its Implications for Politics and Democracy in Nigeria.*
2010. 21 pp. ISBN 978-91-7106-666-4

50. Garth Andrew Myers, *Seven Themes in African Urban Dynamics.*2010. 28 pp.
ISBN 978-91-7106-677-0

51. Abdoumaliq Simone, *The Social Infrastructures of City Life in Contemporary Africa.*
2010. 33 pp. ISBN 978-91-7106-678-7

52. Li Anshan, *Chinese Medical Cooperation in Africa. With Special Emphasis on the Medical Teams and Anti-Malaria Campaign.*
2011. 24 pp. ISBN 978-91-7106-683-1

53. Folashade Hunsu, *Zangbeto: Navigating the Spaces Between Oral art, Communal Security And Conflict Mediation in Badagry, Nigeria.*
2011. 27 pp. ISBN 978-91-7106-688-6

54. Jeremiah O. Arowosegbe, *Reflections on the Challenge of Reconstructing Post-Conflict States in West Africa: Insights from Claude Ake's Political Writings.*
    2011. 40 pp. ISBN 978-91-7106-689-3

55. Bertil Odén, *The Africa Policies of Nordic Countries and the Erosion of the Nordic Aid Model: A comparative study.*
    2011. 66 pp. ISBN 978-91-7106-691-6

56. Angela Meyer, *Peace and Security Cooperation in Central Africa: Developments, Challenges and Prospects.*
    2011. 47 pp ISBN 978-91-7106-693-0